Successful Computing for Business
in a week

Matt Nicholson

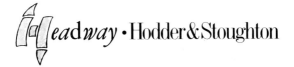

Headway · Hodder & Stoughton

British Library Cataloguing in Publication Data

A record for this title is available from the British Library

ISBN 0 340 62032 3

First published 1994
Impression number 10   9   8   7   6   5   4   3   2   1
Year   1999   1998   1997   1996   1995   1994

Typeset by Multiplex Techniques Ltd, St Mary Cray, Kent.
Printed in Hong Kong for Hodder & Stoughton Educational,
a division of Hodder Headline Plc, 338 Euston Road, London
NW1 3BH by Colorcraft Ltd.

**the Institute
of Management**

F O U N D A T I O N

The Institute of Management (IM) is at the forefront of management development and best management practice. The Institute embraces all levels of management from students to chief executives. It provides a unique portfolio of services for all managers, enabling them to develop skills and achieve management excellence.

For information on the benefits of membership, please contact:

Department HS
Institute of Management
Cottingham Road
Corby
Northants NN17 1TT

Tel. 0536 204222
Fax 0536 201651

This series is commissioned by the Institute of Management Foundation.

C O N T E N T S

Introduction

Information is important to every organisation, whether in the form of purchase orders, sales invoices, economic forecasts, stock prices, interest rates, departure times, exchange rates or climatic conditions. Without the ability to handle information, most organisations would fall apart. Small wonder that information technology, or IT, has become so important to our society.

The main tool that IT makes available is the computer. The modern computer is the ideal tool for sifting, cataloguing, manipulating, presenting, communicating and storing any kind of information. The computer helps us manage the information at our disposal and use it to our benefit, which is what IT is all about.

Like all powerful tools, the computer can do an immense amount of damage if applied in the wrong way. Data is a company's most valuable asset, so you need to proceed cautiously if you intend to commit to a computer system.

Over the next week we will be taking a detailed look at what a computer can do and how it can benefit your business.

Sunday	What is a computer?
Monday	Applications
Tuesday	Behind the scenes
Wednesday	Linking together
Thursday	Buying a system
Friday	Managing a system
Saturday	Preparing for the future

What is a computer?

Computers have become part of our lives. Even if you don't have one on your desk you use one every time you make a phone call, book an airline ticket or go to the bank.

Computers are appearing in our photocopiers, fax machines, televisions and cars. They can be as small as a micro-chip or as large as a room but, almost without exception, they all work in the same way:

Inside the computer
Hardware
- Input and output
- System box
Software
- Applications
- Operating systems

AT THIS STAGE, SHE HAS TO PROVIDE HER OWN SOFTWARE...

Hardware and software

All computers are made up of two important components:
hardware and software. As the name suggests, hardware
refers to the physical bits of plastic, metal and electronics
that make up the machine that we call a 'computer'.
Whatever shape or form it takes, hardware's only purpose is
to do what it is told. Hardware receives instructions from
two sources:

- Its users
- Its software

Of course all machines receive instructions from their users.
Turn on the television and you are giving it an instruction to
display incoming television signals. Press the replay button
on an answerphone and you are telling it to replay the
messages it received while you were out.

The answerphone does this by responding to a set of
instructions built in by its manufacturer, telling it how to go
about the actual process of replaying messages. Such a set of
instructions amounts to a simple 'program' telling the
answerphone how to respond when you press the replay
button. Most modern gadgets have such programs built into
them, telling them how to carry out the instructions they
receive from their users:

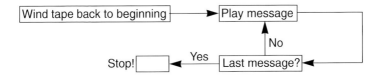

The answerphone, like most machines, has this program built in to its hardware. You can decide whether to press the replay button or not, but you cannot influence what happens when you do.

This is where the computer is unique. With a computer, these programs are not built into the hardware, but instead are stored in a more mutable form. What is more, you can change the way that your computer works simply by changing its program.

This mutability has led to computer programs being called 'software'. Computer hardware is simply a tool for running software programs. It is the software that makes the computer do something useful. If you run a word-processor program, your computer becomes a tool for writing letters and reports. If you run a design program, it becomes a tool for creating drawings and pictures.

The letters, reports and drawings that you work on represent the data. A computer system is simply a tool for manipulating data, and in most businesses the data is far more valuable than both the hardware and the software put together. You can always replace a computer and its software, but replacing a year's sales figures is another matter altogether.

Tomorrow we will look at just a few of the many tasks that software can make your computer perform. Today, we will concentrate on the hardware.

Input and output

Computers come in all shapes and sizes: however, standard personal or desktop computers have a number of features in common:

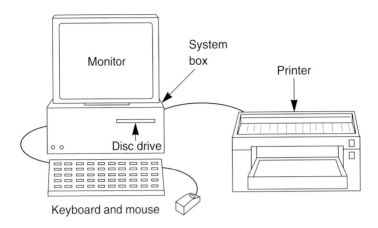

With the exception of the system box, all these components
are concerned with input and output. Most office computers
are controlled through a keyboard and mouse, and most
output their results to a monitor or a printer.

The keyboard
The keyboard is a tried and tested way to input words and
numbers, and most computer keyboards do indeed include
a section which looks exactly like a conventional typewriter.

Computer keyboards also have 'control' and 'function' keys
which many computer programs allow you to assign to
common operations. This means that you can trigger quite
complicated responses with a single keystroke. Most
keyboards also include a set of keys laid out to look like a
calculator, called a 'numeric keypad'.

The mouse
A more modern input device is the mouse. This can be
linked through software to a pointer on the screen so that
the pointer matches the movements you make with the

mouse on your desk. There is also a button on the mouse which you can use to mark your position, a process known as 'clicking'.

The mouse is the ideal tool for controlling a drawing or painting application, where you can use it almost as you would a paintbrush. It is also useful for making selections from the screen or marking blocks of text.

Other input devices
The mouse and keyboard are the most common input devices, however, there are other gadgets that you can use to control your computer. Instead of a mouse you can use a pen and a special touch-pad, and indeed many feel that a pen gives finer control. Combined with handwriting-recognition software, you can even use the pen as a writing tool.

If you are involved in graphic design you may find a scanner useful. This scans printed images and converts them into electrical signals that the computer can work with. Alternatively you can link your computer to electrical transducers so that it can respond automatically to changes in temperature or speed or whatever else the transducer is designed to measure.

The monitor
The computer also needs to communicate with you, either to present you with the results of its computations or to ask you for further information. This is usually done through the monitor, a television-like device on which software programs display both text and graphics.

The standard desktop computer comes with a monitor that does indeed work like a television, displaying its images on a 12 or 14 inch screen. Those involved in graphic design may want a larger screen, and it is possible to buy monitors capable of displaying whole A4 or A3 page at a time. Many publishing companies use such screens for designing magazine and newspaper pages.

Portable computers are at the opposite extreme as they require a screen that is both small and light. Here liquid crystal displays are common, which work in exactly the same way as the LCD display on a digital watch. Liquid crystal displays tend to have a low contrast image which responds rather slowly to changes. Rather better are active matrix displays as these give a brighter image and a faster response.

The printer
Images on a screen are transient. More often than not you want the end result printed out on paper (or 'hard copy', as it is known in the trade).

Dot matrix printers used to be the most common type of printer, but nowadays they are seldom seen outside the warehouse or the factory floor where ruggedness is more important than print quality. In the office they have largely been superseded by laser printers, primarily because the laser printer can consistently produce black and white images of a high quality, and is much quieter.

A cheaper alternative is the ink-jet printer. These can produce high quality results but tend to be slower than the laser printer and less consistent. Nevertheless, colour ink-jet printers are the cheapest way of producing acceptable colour print.

Other output devices
A variant on the printer is the plotter, commonly used by architects and draughtsmen to produce precision line drawings. Alternatively the computer can be connected to almost any type of machine, and indeed the modern desktop computer is quite capable of controlling a whole production line or even a factory.

The system box

So far we've looked at those parts of the computer which are concerned only with input and output. Now it's time to look inside the box that sits in between. The most important component here is the central processing unit, or CPU, which is responsible for actually executing the instructions that make up a program.

As far as the CPU is concerned, everything is expressed as numbers. You may type words on the keyboard, but the electronics behind the keyboard translates each character into a numeric code. When the computer displays a picture, the image is represented internally as a set of numeric values. These values are transformed into an image by electronic circuitry both inside the system unit and inside the monitor. Even the instructions that make up the computer program itself are expressed as numbers.

The CPU essentially consists of two components: the processor, which can loosely be compared to the human brain; and the memory, which serves a similar function to our own memory. The processor carries out the actual calculations while the values on which it works, the instructions that make up the program and the data on which the program acts, are stored in memory.

Imagine that you have been asked to calculate the monthly payments on a loan. You have been given a pencil and paper so the first thing you do is write down the relevant factors, such as the amount and period of the loan and the current interest rate, together with the formula that derives the payment from these factors. This formula will require a number of intermediary calculations before you get the final result, and you write the results of these calculations on the paper as you go.

Here the paper is serving the same function as the computer's memory. Not only does it store the data required for this particular calculation, but it also stores the formula used for the calculation which is analogous to the program itself.

The processor
The modern micro-processor is one of the miracles of the twentieth century. This is a complete processor unit on a single microchip. The chip is housed in a plastic case but inside is a tiny sliver of silicon perhaps a centimetre across containing literally millions of transistors and capable of performing literally millions of calculations each second. We will be looking at the processor in more depth on Tuesday.

The memory
In an ideal world a computer's memory would have an unlimited capacity, would be able to store and recall data almost instantaneously, would retain its contents come what may, and would cost virtually nothing. In practice, no single technology can satisfy all these criteria so computers use different technologies for different purposes.

The result is a hierarchy of storage devices, with the fastest and most expensive nearest the processor and the slowest and cheapest further away. Data is moved from one to the other as it is needed:

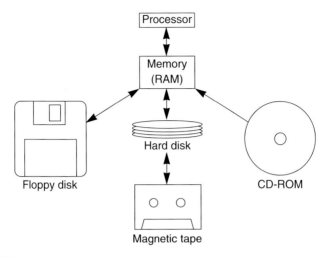

Kilobytes and megabytes

Before we look in detail at these memory devices, we need to understand how their capacity is expressed. As we saw earlier, both program instructions and data are stored as numeric codes. These codes are not expressed in the decimal form that we use but as binary numbers, using just the characters zero and one.

Just as decimal numbers are expressed in terms of digits, so binary numbers are expressed in 'bits'. Large binary values are usually divided into 8-bit chunks called 'bytes', and the capacity of a memory device is normally expressed in terms of the number of bytes that it can store.

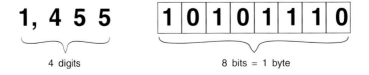

These days, most devices can store thousands or even millions of bytes at a time, which is where the term 'kilobyte' and 'megabyte' come in. However because the computer uses binary arithmetic, these expressions do not have quite the same meaning as they would in decimal arithmetic:

1 kilobyte (1K) = 1 024 bytes
1 megabyte (1Mb) = 1 024K = 1 048 576 bytes

To give you some idea of what these figures mean in real life, a single page of type containing around 500 words would require a little over three kilobytes of storage space. The text in a fairly hefty paperback, or a handful of TV-quality images, would require in the region of one megabyte.

Memory or RAM

The fastest type of memory is Random Access Memory, or RAM for short, which is constructed from silicon chips. The major problem with RAM is that its contents are lost as soon as the power is removed.

Some portable computers use batteries to maintain power to RAM even when the rest of the computer is turned off, but in general RAM is used for temporary storage. Programs and data are usually held on a more permanent medium and copied or 'loaded' into RAM just before the program is run. Most modern computers have a least 4Mb of RAM.

Hard disk drive

The programs and data that you use day-to-day are usually stored on a hard disk. The hard disk stores data magnetically, in much the same way as a tape recorder. Instead of a strip of magnetic tape, the hard disk uses a set of magnetic disks that are stacked one above the other and rotated at high speed.

Hard disks are considerably slower than silicon chips; however, they do maintain their content after the power is turned off. They are also far cheaper and better adapted to storing large quantities of data. Most modern desktop computers contain hard disks with a capacity of at least 100Mb, and sometimes considerably more.

Floppy disks
The ideal medium for carrying programs and data about is the floppy disk. The floppy disk works in the same way as the hard disk, recording data magnetically onto a rotating disk that is protected by a plastic case. However the disk rotates at a slower speed, which means that it takes longer to access, and it stores much less data.

The floppy disk is also removable, which means that you can take one disk out of the floppy disk drive and put in another. In this sense it works much like an audio cassette.

Most modern floppy disks are 3.5 inches in diameter and store either 720K or 1.44Mb of data. Although they are too slow for everyday storage, they are ideal for keeping a copy of your data away from the computer itself. For this reason they are often used for 'backing up' your hard disk, ensuring you have a copy of any important information should anything go wrong with your hard disk.

Magnetic tape
Conventional magnetic tape is not used as a primary means of storage these days because it is too slow. However its capacity does make it ideal as a backup medium.

Backing up onto floppy disk means swapping tens or even hundreds of floppy disks in and out of the floppy disk drive. The alternative is to use special tape cartridges each capable of storing several hundred megabytes. It may still take quite a time to copy across your data but at least it can be done automatically, without you around.

CD-ROM
The ideal medium for storing large amounts of data is the CD-ROM, short for Compact Disc Read Only Memory. A CD-ROM is just like an audio CD, except that it holds up to 650Mb of computer data, rather than music. The disks are 'read-only' like an audio CD but, as with an audio CD player, a single CD-ROM drive can be used to read as many CD-ROMs as you want.

CD-ROMs are the reference books of the computer world, ideal for bringing you large amounts of information about a particular topic. Their capacity makes them particularly well suited for storing pictures and even video sequences.

Summary

Having reached the end of Sunday you should now have some understanding of the following points:

- That computers run 'programs'
- The difference between the hardware and software
- The role played by the processor
- The role played by the computer's memory

We have also looked at various devices that can be used for:

- Getting information into the computer
- Extracting information from the computer
- Storing programs and data for later use

Applications

By itself, a computer is nothing but an expensive paperweight. As we saw yesterday, computers are totally useless without software. It is the software that turns the computer into a powerful writing tool, storage system or calculating machine. Only when you have installed suitable software onto its hard disk can it take an active role in your business.

This type of software is known as 'application' software because it allows you to use the computer for a specific job. Underneath the applications is another layer of software called the 'operating system' which acts as an intermediary between the application and the hardware itself. Tomorrow we will look at operating systems in more depth: today we will concentrate on applications.

There is a vast range of application software available off the shelf, enabling the computer to perform almost any task you could imagine. Thankfully, most applications fall into three main categories.

- General purpose applications
- Graphics software
- Office tools

If you don't find an application package off the shelf that suits your company's needs, you can always have it tailor-made. This costs more but can be worth while in the long run. Many applications also include 'macro' languages which can be used to adapt the way that the application works.

We will be covering the commissioning of software development on Thursday but meanwhile, let's look at the main types of software available.

General purpose applications

Word processing, spreadsheets and database management are the mainstay of any computer system, and always have been. People were using dedicated word processors before the personal computer appeared, and it was arguably *VisiCalc*, the first spreadsheet program, that encouraged the business world to take personal computers seriously. Databases were being run on some of the earliest computers ever built, and indeed many large businesses still rely on the company mainframe to handle their main database systems.

Word processing
The word processor has revolutionised the way that offices handle letters, reports and other such documents. With a word processor you can make major changes to your text

without having to throw it all away and start from scratch, and that feature alone has rendered the office typewriter almost completely redundant.

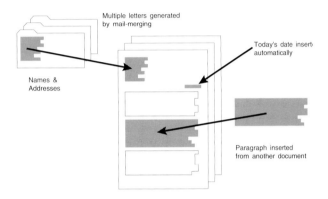

Multiple letters generated by mail-merging

Today's date inserte automatically

Names & Addresses

Paragraph inserted from another document

Whole documents can be assembled by cutting or copying words, sentences or whole paragraphs from one document and pasting them into another. Most word processors also support mail-merge so that you can send the same letter to many different people, substituting relevant information into the text where required. Using mail-merge you could, for example, have a standard reminder letter sent automatically to any account overdue by more than 90 days, and have the amount owed inserted into the appropriate point in the text.

Modern word processors provide a host of additional tools aimed at both standard office use and the professional writer, many encroaching into the facilities normally associated with full-blown desktop publishing. Particularly useful is the ability to create standard templates that establish the overall appearance of the document, using layout and typography to establish an identifying style.

Spreadsheets

Spreadsheet software is the ideal tool for budgeting and forecasting, or indeed any job that requires the manipulation of large tables filled with figures. What makes a spreadsheet so powerful is that each cell in a spreadsheet table can contain not just text or numbers, but also formulae whose values are automatically kept up to date. Change a figure in one cell and all the formulae which reference that cell are instantly recalculated so that the whole spreadsheet reflects the change:

	A	B	C	D
1		Quantity	Price	Total
2	January	450	£82.00	B2*C2
3	February	360	£85.00	B3*C3
4	March	380	£90.00	B4*C4
5	First Quarter			SUM(D2..D4)

A modern spreadsheet can do in seconds what would take a whole team of people many hours or even days to duplicate. This makes it possible to tinker with the values, trying out 'what-if' scenarios until you get the result you want. Many spreadsheets even support 'goal seeking', effectively reversing the process so as to calculate the initial values required for a particular bottom line. Most also allow you to generate graphs from the tabular information, usually in a wide range of styles.

Database management

While word processors and spreadsheets are extremely useful, the core of most businesses revolves around a database. Book a railway journey, a theatre ticket or hotel room and the chances are that your booking has been recorded in a database. Designing a database system that reflects the real needs of a business, both now and in the future, can be crucial to a business's survival.

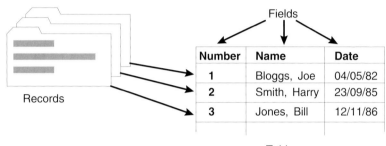

Table

At one level a database is simply an electronic card box. Each card in the box constitutes a 'record' and the various categories of data recorded on each card – name, address, telephone number, and so forth – constitute the 'fields'. The whole collection of records is referred to as a 'table'.

This kind of database is called a 'flat file' database, and is inherently very limited. If you were to use a single table to store invoice details, for example, each record would need to store not only the details of each order but also the name and address of each customer. Ten different orders placed by the same customer would mean entering the same name and address ten times, which is both inefficient and unreliable.

A better solution is to store the customers' names and addresses in one table and the order details in another. The two tables can then be linked through a common field or 'primary key', such as a customer ID number. The primary key allows you to link order details from one table with customer details from another, providing the information you need to generate an invoice.

Customer table

No	Name	Company	Phone
1	Bloggs, Joe	Bloggs & Co	0919 996 567
2	Smith, Bob	Widgets Limited	0929 994 126

Order table

Quantity	Item	Supplier
145	4-inch woggles	2
163	medium widgets	2
24	4lb hammers	1

Invoice

Bob Smith
Widgets Limited   0929 994 126

145   4-inch woggles
163   medium widgets

This method of handling data is called the 'relational database model' and is by far the most important in use today. The software that maintains the database tables and provides you with the tools to manipulate them is called a Database Management System, or DBMS.

Accounting software

Although perceived as a different category, an accounting package is essentially a DBMS which has been tailored to a specific purpose. The various ledgers used to maintain a company's accounts are well suited to the relational database model, and indeed many software publishers sell accounting packages that have been constructed using an off-the-shelf DBMS.

Mainstream accounting systems tend to be sold as a suite of modules that can be used together in various combinations:

Core modules
- Sales ledger
- Purchase ledger
- Nominal ledger

Optional modules
- Invoicing
- Payroll
- Stock control
- Job costing
- Asset management
- Budget management
- Management reports

The simplest accounting packages are the personal banking systems which allow you to track separate cheque book, cash and credit card accounts, and not much else. One step up from these is the 'cashbook' system which offers you the computer equivalent of a general or nominal ledger, allowing you to categorise transactions and deal with VAT.

It is important that a company chooses an accounting suite that is both sympathetic to its current practices and flexible enough to cope with future growth.

Integrated suites
Many publishers bundle word processor, spreadsheet and database manager into a single package, adding facilities that allow you to move data from one module to another. This means that you can integrate the output from each module into a single document, producing letters and reports that include graphs generated by the spreadsheet and data values taken from the database.

As we shall see on Tuesday, operating environments such as Windows allow this sort of integration between ordinary application software, which effectively renders purpose-built integrated suites redundant. Currently, the trend is to bundle modules which are less powerful than their stand-alone equivalents. Nevertheless they often provide all the basic facilities that you actually need and are usually very easy to use, which can make them very good value.

Graphics software

In the early days, most computer software fell into one of the categories discussed above. More recently, the development of high resolution displays and printers and the ever-increasing power of the desktop computer has made it a viable tool for graphic work as well.

As a result, publishers, designers, artists and draughtsman are increasingly turning to the computer rather than more traditional tools such as the pencil, airbrush and set square.

Image editing versus drawing

Computers handle graphic images in two ways. On the one hand they can treat the image as a mosaic of coloured dots, much like the dots that are used to make up newspaper and magazine pictures. This pattern of dots is called a 'bit map' because each dot is represented in the computer by binary numbers whose value determines its colour.

Alternatively the image can be treated as a collection of discrete objects, such as lines, squares, circles and polygons. Each shape can be defined mathematically; a rectangle by the coordinates of its corners, a circle by its radius and the position of its centre, and so on. These are referred to as 'vector' images because they are largely built up of vectors joining one point to another.

Bit-mapped image · · · · · · · · · · · · · · · · · Vector image

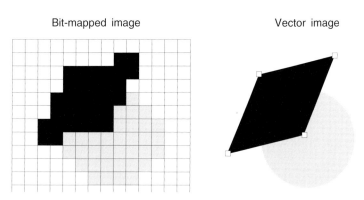

Which you use depends on the type of work you are doing. Bit-maps are best suited to real-life images such as those produced by a scanner or a digitising camera. The pictures stored on a Photo CD, for example, are bit-mapped images. Packages for editing bit-mapped images are described as 'painting' or, for the most sophisticated, 'image editing' packages.

Vector images are better suited to abstract pictures, although a professional designer can create very realistic effects by using a large number of objects. Software for creating vector images is generally referred to as 'drawing' software, or at the top end of the market, CAD which is short for Computer Aided Design. CAD software is particularly geared to high-precision architectural and technical drawing.

Vector images are inherently more precise than bit-mapped images and have the advantage of keeping each object distinct from its neighbours. In the vector diagram above, for example, you would be able to move the black diamond away from the circle very easily, simply by selecting it with your mouse and dragging it to its new position. The same effect would be almost impossible to achieve with the bit-mapped version.

Desktop publishing
In the mid-1980s, desktop publishing swept through the publishing industry to such an extent that few news-stand magazines are now produced using traditional methods. DTP, as it is also known, provides all the tools you need to produce professional publications from a desktop computer. Typical features that you would expect from a DTP package include:

- Creating a multi-column 'grid' for the page
- Accepting text from a wide range of word processors that can be 'flowed' into the columns
- Accepting both bit-mapped and vector graphics that can be positioned on the page wherever required
- Ensuring that the text flows around the pictures correctly

- Support for a wide range of typefaces (or 'fonts') and typographic effects
- Precise control over the size and spacing of the characters
- Output of colour separations as required by commercial printers

Whilst most DTP packages are capable of professional results, the end result is limited by the capabilities of current desktop scanners and laser printers. Professional quality colour scanners and high resolution image setters are only financially viable for those actually in the publishing industry. For most of us, it makes more sense to use a typsetting bureau.

This means that you can use your own laser printer to print proof copies, but take the final pages along to the bureau where they can be professionally typeset on a per-page basis. Many bureaux also have colour scanning facilities and can supply you with bit-mapped images of your pictures which you can use with your DTP software.

Presentation graphics

A presentation package effectively does for slide-show presentations what DTP does for printed publications. Using presentation software you can take images and text from various sources and combine them into a set of images designed to be displayed one after the other like a slide show. Presentation packages are particularly adept at turning spreadsheet data into attractive charts, suitably annotated and embellished.

Most presentation packages can emulate the dissolves and fades that you would expect from a real slide show, which means that you can run your presentation directly from the screen of your computer. For larger audiences you can either use special projectors that can be driven directly from computer's monitor connector, or you can convert the screen images into 35mm slides using special equipment. Again, most companies find it more cost efficient to use a bureau that can carry out such conversions on a per-slide basis.

Office tools

Of the countless other types of application packages available, there are three further categories that merit a mention in the space available here. These categories are concerned with general office management and have become increasingly important as tools for 'workgroup computing', which we will be covering on Wednesday.

Project management

Once a project grows above a certain size it becomes a full-time job tracking who's supposed to be doing what, making sure each team has the resources for the job, and keeping tabs on the escalating cost. Project management software enables you to divide a project into tasks, each allocated its own resources and start and end times, so that you can keep track of its progress and spot problems before they arise.

Personal information managers
PIMs, as they are also called, are an attempt to computerise the assorted diaries, address books, notepads and to-do lists that clutter our desks. Closely related are 'contact manager' programs that are more specifically aimed at telephone call management.

Document image processing
Despite promises of a paperless office, most companies are still beset by paper documents. 'Document image processing' or DIP systems are concerned with transferring such documentation onto computer, either as scanned images or as text data, and cataloguing it for archival purposes.

Converting a typewritten or printed document into a computer file requires additional OCR or 'optical character recognition' software, and is far from an exact science. Often it is sufficient merely to store the document as a scanned bit-map image that can be printed out or viewed on screen if it is ever needed.

Summary

Today we have concentrated on application software, looking at just a few of the many tasks that you can accomplish with the aid of a computer:

- Word processing
- Financial analysis and forecasting
- Storing and manipulating data
- Keeping accounts
- Creating and editing images
- Desktop publishing
- Designing and delivering presentations
- Project planning
- Managing personal information

Behind the scenes

As we saw on Sunday, computer software consists of many thousands of instructions, each ready to be executed by the computer's central processor. Unfortunately not all processors understand the same set of instructions, so a computer program will only run on the processor for which it was written. Obviously, it is very important that you choose a computer that uses the right processor for the software you intend to use. To this end, we will look at the following today:

- Operating systems
- Architectures
- Processors

Operating systems

For computer software, running on foreign hardware is not unlike finding yourself in a foreign country. It's hard to make yourself understood if you don't speak the local language, and telephone systems generate unfamiliar sounds, for example, making it difficult to make a phone call.

In the same way, not all printers understand the same set of instructions, or send back the same messages, so a program designed to print through one model may not be able to print through another. Not all computers use the same method of storing data either, so a program could find itself unable to retrieve vital information on a foreign machine.

Indeed in the early days, when there weren't very many computers to choose between, each application was written not just for a particular processor, but to run on a specific model of computer. Thankfully, as the computer industry expanded, someone came up with the idea of an 'operating system'.

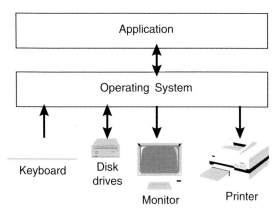

The operating system is a special program that hides the idiosyncrasies of the hardware from the application. It allows the application to control the various hardware components through a uniform interface, regardless of make or model. If the application needs to use a particular component it can pass the operating system a simple command, rather than talk directly to the component itself.

It is as if you were provided with an assistant for your foreign trip, someone who not only speaks the language but also understands the vagaries of the local telephone system. Rather than battle with the telephone yourself you can ask the assistant to put the call through, and let you know when the connection has been successfully made.

The personal assistant or secretary is a good analogy here. To take the analogy further, most companies find it more efficient to have a core of such people providing basic office services, so that those involved in more specific tasks need not concern themselves with the details when it comes to making phone calls, managing the post and so forth. In the same way, the computer industry has found it more efficient to handle the basic tasks of printing, managing storage systems and so forth, through a common operating system. We will look at operating systems in more detail later today.

Architectures

Nowadays, computer hardware has settled into a number of important 'architectures'. Computers that fall within a particular architecture use hardware components – disk drives, monitors and so forth – that work in the same way and can be controlled using the same electrical signals. Some architectures are proprietary, surviving because they satisfy a particular need in the market. Others are openly available to third parties wishing to use the design for their own models, although this may involve a licensing arrangement with the original designer.

As we shall see, each architecture is based around a particular family of processors, and has attracted its own set of operating systems. As you would expect, there are close relationships between the principle companies involved, although these are not always trouble-free!

Processors

Despite the different instruction sets, all processors essentially perform the same task: executing the instructions required by your computer software. The speed with which the software runs depends to a large extent on the speed of the processor, which in turn depends on three factors:

- Clock rate (measured in MHz)
- Processing efficiency
- Bus widths (measured in bits)

Clock rate

Most processors are 'clocked' which means that their operations are synchronised to the beat of an electronic clock. This clock emits many millions of pulses each second, so its speed is usually expressed in Megahertz, or MHz for short. Speeds of 33 or 66MHz are common.

Processing efficiency

This does not mean that a whole instruction is executed for each clock beat. Most instructions take several operations to complete, depending on their complexity, so another important factor is the efficiency with which each instruction is processed. Most processors these days use a 'pipeline', for example, using production-line techniques to process more than one instruction at a time.

Bus width

Another factor affecting the speed of computation is the amount of data that can be processed by each instruction. This is determined by the number of bits that the processor can handle at a time. At the time of writing most computers use 32-bit processors, although 64-bit processors are becoming common.

There are literally hundreds of different processors on the market today, however those that you are likely to find inside a personal computer divide into three groups, each associated with a particular range of architectures:

Intel x86 processors
- PC compatible architecture

Motorola 680x0 processors
- Apple Macintosh architecture

RISC processors
- Sun SPARCStations
- Hewlett Packard's PA-RISC range
- IBM RS/6000 range
- IBM and Apple PowerPC range
- DEC Alpha PC range
- Silicon Graphics Indigo range

Intel and the IBM PC

It was at Intel that the micro-processor was first invented, so it is perhaps not surprising that Intel processors dominate the personal computer world today. In fact Intel's success in this field is largely down to IBM, which chose the Intel 8088 processor for one of its first personal computers, the IBM PC.

IBM has a history going back to before the Second World War, and dominated the computer market until the mid-1980s. The original IBM PC, launched in 1981, was little more than a hobbyist's toy, however the letters 'IBM' ensured that it would be taken seriously by the business community.

Furthermore, IBM had been in such a hurry to produce the PC that it had used largely third-party components, which meant that its architecture was fairly open. Shortly after its release the first 'clones' appeared, machines made by other manufacturers that were similar enough to the IBM PC to run the same software.

By the mid-1980s, the majority of personal computers were 'PC-compatible', although vastly more powerful than the original PC. This was possible because Intel ensured that all its subsequent processors remained compatible with the original 8088, right through to the i486 and Pentium processors available today.

Motorola and the Apple Mac
At the time of the IBM PC's launch, its main competitor was made by Apple. In 1984, while everyone else was busy building PC-compatibles, Apple produced a radical new computer called the Macintosh or 'Mac' for short.

The Macintosh was anything but PC compatible. Its main selling point was that it was much easier to use, being the first computer to come with a mouse and an operating system controlled from a graphical user interface.

A year later Apple launched the LaserWriter, the first desktop laser printer, which gave the Macintosh a huge advantage when it came to graphics applications. Indeed in the 1980s the Apple Macintosh was the only sensible choice for a desktop publishing system.

Much of the Macintosh's power came from its 68000 processor, made by Motorola. Over the years the Macintosh has graduated up to the 68040 processor and is now moving on to the PowerPC, which is a RISC processor.

RISC chips
While Intel and Motorola's processors currently dominate the mainstream business market, a range of more powerful processors have become established in the specialist graphics market. These come under the general heading of RISC processors, which stands for Reduced Instruction Set Computers.

As the name suggests, RISC processors support a more limited range of simpler instructions than those discussed so far. Because of their simpler design, RISC processors can run at far higher clock speeds than the Intel x86 or Motorola 68000 ranges, and have the potential to offer far greater performance.

Until recently, RISC processors have primarily been associated with high-power graphics workstations, such as Sun's SPARCStation and the Indigo range from Silicon Graphics. However the PowerPC range of processors is the result of a collaboration between IBM and Motorola and, like the DEC Alpha, is beginning to make an impact on the more mainstream business market.

Operating systems in detail

There are many different types of operating systems, however, most are made up of the same basic components. At their heart is the 'kernel'. This is principally concerned with allocating memory and processor time to applications, and providing an interface to the hardware.

The hardware itself is generally controlled through 'device drivers'. These are programs written specifically to match a particular device, such as a printer or a monitor, to the operating system. Separating them from the main kernel means that they can easily be replaced: buy a new printer and you can use it with your existing operating system simply by installing the appropriate printer driver.

One of the most important functions of an operating system is the management of data storage. This is usually achieved by storing documents and programs in 'files' that are each given a unique name. These files are usually grouped into 'directories' which perform a similar function to the dividers that you might use in a conventional filing cabinet.

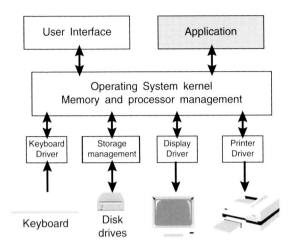

Lastly, there is the user interface. This is the 'face' of the operating system providing us with the tools we need to control the computer. It is through the user interface that we start applications running, copy files from one storage medium to another, and carry out general housekeeping tasks.

Operating systems fall into three main categories:

- Single user
- Multi-tasking
- Multi-user

A single-user operating system is designed to run just one application at a time. Imagine that you need to consult a spreadsheet in the middle of writing a report. With a single-user operating system you would have to close down the word processor, load up the spreadsheet, jot down the relevant information, and then close down the spreadsheet and reload the word processor before you can continue.

A multi-tasking operating system on the other hand, is capable of looking after more than one application at the same time. Here you would be able to load up your spreadsheet and find the necessary figures without having to close down your word processor. Indeed most multi-tasking operating systems provide mechanisms that allow you to transfer data automatically from one application to another.

A multi-user operating system adds further facilities so that more than one user can operate the system at the same time. In particular, a multi-user system should provide password protection so that each user can be allocated a private storage area. There also needs to be a mechanism for handling users that want to make changes to the same document at the same time.

We will be looking at these issues in more detail tomorrow. In the meantime, let's look at the main operating systems currently in use.

DOS
When IBM launched the PC it also needed an operating system. Rather than write one of its own, it went to Microsoft, who produced the Microsoft Disk Operating System, or MS-DOS for short, which IBM bundled with the PC under the name PC-DOS.

Other manufacturers were able to ensure compatibility by bundling their PCs with MS-DOS. As a result DOS, as it is generically known, is used on more computers than any other operating system.

This is a simple single-user operating system and is now decidedly out-dated. For a start, it can only directly use the first 640K of memory in your machine and it also has a primitive user interface which requires you to type complicated instructions on the keyboard.

It has survived this long simply because of the number of applications written for it. Various attempts have been made to enhance DOS, both by giving it a more advanced user interface and by tricking it into accessing more than 640K of memory through special programs called 'DOS extenders'. The most successful DOS extender was Microsoft's own Windows, which has now become an operating system in its own right.

Apple Macintosh
The main reason for the success of the Apple Macintosh is its operating system. In stark contrast to the PC, the

Macintosh has a user interface that employs graphics rather than text-based instructions, and is controlled by a mouse.

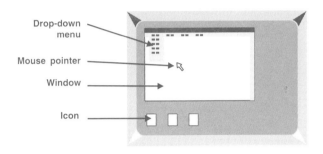

Drop-down menu
Mouse pointer
Window
Icon

The principle elements of the Macintosh user interface are its windows, icons and drop-down menus. These are manipulated through the mouse pointer, an arrow that moves around the screen as you move the mouse around your desk. Activate an icon by 'double-clicking' it with the mouse, and the associated document appears in a window on screen, ready-loaded into the appropriate application. The application itself can then be controlled by making selections from menus that drop down from the 'menu bar'.

Ordinary people find the Macintosh's interface much easier to understand than DOS's arcane one. It also lends itself to running more than one application at once as each can be given its own window, and indeed modern versions are fully multi-tasking.

Windows
Microsoft's reaction to the Mac was Windows. This started life as a DOS program that provided a graphic user interface similar to the Macintosh and some multi-tasking facilities.

Microsoft was very careful to ensure that Windows could successfully multi-task DOS applications while cultivating a market for more sophisticated Windows applications. As a result, Windows now dominates the personal computer world.

Windows has also become an operating system in its own right, with successive versions taking over more and more of the tasks previously handled by DOS. It is a fully multi-tasking operating system and has sophisticated mechanisms for creating 'compound documents', or single documents that contain elements created by a number of different application packages. As we shall see tomorrow, it also offers many of the facilities necessary for networking.

OS/2

Originally a joint venture between Microsoft and IBM, OS/2 was the companies' first attempt to build a better operating system for the PC than DOS. Microsoft pulled out of the project when Windows became successful, but IBM continued development. As a result, OS/2 now competes with Windows.

OS/2 offers much the same facilities as Windows and is capable of running both DOS and Windows applications as well as those written specifically to run under OS/2. Indeed, it can offer a more secure way of running some Windows applications than Windows itself, but it does require rather more memory and disk space than a comparable Windows system.

Unix

Older than any of the operating systems we've covered so far is Unix, a true multi-user system written for the minicomputers of the 1970s. Although there are versions available for the PC, these days Unix is principally to be found on minicomputers and RISC-based workstations.

Summary

Having reached the end of our third day you should now have a useful perspective on the different types of computer available, and on the relationship between the operating system and the processor. In particular we have covered:

Architectures
- Intel processors and the IBM PC
- Motorola and Apple
- Systems based on RISC chips

Operating Systems
- MS-DOS and PC-DOS
- The Apple Macintosh
- Microsoft Windows
- IBM's OS/2
- Unix

Linking together

So far we have treated the personal computer largely as a tool that helps individual users do their jobs. Link their computers together, though, and you can help them work better as a group, creating a network that lets them share information and resources. This is 'workgroup computing' and it is facilitated by 'groupware', a class of application specifically designed for people working in groups.

Connect your computer to the telephone system and you can link into computer networks anywhere in the world. This not only gives you access to vast amounts of information, but also allows you to trade electronically with other companies.

Workgroup computing and computer-based telecommunications have the potential to transform your business beyond recognition. Handled correctly they could give your business a real competitive edge. Handle these technologies badly, or not at all, and you could soon fall by the wayside.

Today, we will examine these ways of using computers and look at how they can help you in your business:

- Networking systems
- Workgroup computing
- Communications

Networking systems

There are two principal ways in which you can link users through computers:

- Multi-user systems
- Networked systems

Multi-user systems

In a multi-user system, each user is allocated a terminal that is connected to a single, central computer. The terminals have no intrinsic computing power themselves, simply providing a keyboard for data input and a screen for display. For this reason they are often referred to as 'dumb' terminals. All the processing power resides with the central machine which would be running a multi-user operating system such as Unix.

Such systems have a number of disadvantages. For a start, the performance of each terminal is directly dependent on the number connected; add further terminals and the performance of each one deteriorates. Secondly, if the central computer malfunctions, the whole system becomes useless.

Networked systems

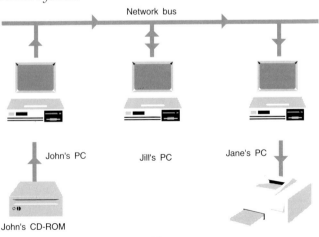

Rather more flexible is the local area network or LAN. Here there is no central computer. Instead each user has his or her own computer which communicates with the others through the linking cable. Computing power is concentrated with the users and the network is used simply to transfer data that needs to flow from one user's computer to another. This means much less traffic and potentially a much faster system.

Peer-to-peer networks
Networks allow users to share resources. It makes little sense for everyone in a company to have their own laser printer, but with a network, a single laser printer can be shared amongst several people. In the example above, Jill can read files from John's CD-ROM and print them out on Jane's laser printer, while both Jane and John can access files on Jill's hard disk.

This is achieved through a set of software programs that together make up a network operating system:

- Client software
- File server software
- Print server software
- Communications server software
- Network communications software and drivers

Computers that make use of network resources are called 'clients', while the computers that supply the resources are called 'servers'. For a machine to access a server it has to be running suitable client software, and for a machine to make its peripherals available it must run the appropriate server software.

A machine can run both client and server software at the same time, as indeed all three machines are doing in the example above. In addition, every computer on the network needs to run network communications software and the appropriate drivers for the network hardware in order to communicate with the network at all.

This sort of network is called a 'peer-to-peer' network because each computer has the same status and can potentially offer the same services. Peer-to-peer networking has become very popular and is now an integral part of many operating systems.

Client/server systems

Having someone else use your printer or access your hard disk requires the attention of your computer, and will temporarily slow down its operation. For this reason peer-to-peer systems are only practical for a limited number of users. Larger networks work better if one or more machines are designated as file servers, providing a central source for shared data and resources. Such systems are also easier to manage because all important data is stored in a single location.

Allocating a machine as a dedicated file server means that it can be built with file serving in mind. For a start, it need not run the same operating system as client machines, but instead something designed specifically to allow fast multi-user access to very large hard disks. The most common server operating system in use today is NetWare from Novell, although both Microsoft and IBM offer alternatives in Windows NT Advanced Server and OS/2 LAN Server.

Distributed applications

A client/server system is in many ways a halfway house between peer-to-peer networking and the old-fashioned multi-user system, and has the potential to offer the best of both.

In a conventional multi-user system, applications run on the central computer itself which means a lot of network traffic as each workstation's screen is kept up to date. In a client/server system, applications are run on the client machines and can be stored either on the client's hard disk or on the file server. Either way, only document files need traverse the network once the application is loaded.

Distributed applications take this idea further by splitting the application into two parts, one running on the client machine and the other on the server itself. This technique is particularly useful in database management where the client or 'front end' makes requests of the 'database engine', a separate 'back-end' program running on the file server.

If the client requires information about one particular record, the database engine can process this request and return just the data that matches the criteria. This is far more efficient than a conventional system where the whole database file would need to traverse the network.

Structured Query Language or SQL has become the standard means of communication between client applications and database servers. Any application can control an SQL server by sending it instructions written in SQL.

Workgroup computing

Although the distinction is somewhat tenuous, workgroup computing is generally taken to mean groups working within a single organisation, as opposed to 'wide area' networks that involve communication links to outside organisations. This doesn't necessarily mean that all the members of the group need to be in the same building, or even in the same country, but has more to do with the needs of the group itself.

At the group level, there are several different ways in which a network can bring benefits to an organisation.

- Electronic mail
- Sharing documents
- Conferencing
- Electronic form management

Electronic mail

On a larger network, spread across several rooms or buildings, electronic mail becomes useful. E-mail, as it is more usually called, works in much the same way as conventional mail. Each user on the network is allocated a code, called a 'mailbox' address, that identifies a private storage area on the system. E-mail software lets users read messages addressed to them and send messages to other users on the network.

E-mail combines the advantages of both the telephone system and the mail. Like the telephone it provides an instant means of communication, but like the mail it allows users to respond in their own time, rather than the instant it arrives. It also overcomes 'telephone tag', that game which involves leaving countless messages for someone, only to be away from your desk or making another call when they finally get back to you.

Most e-mail software allows you to attach files to your messages that have been produced using other applications.

E-mail then becomes an efficient way of sending whole documents, or indeed any other type of data, around an organisation.

Sharing documents

A computer network allows more than one person to contribute to the same document, making amendments and adding comments to other people's work. Most conventional applications can be used in this way but there are hidden dangers. It is very easy to lose track of who made which changes, for example, and all too easy to end up with the wrong version of an important document.

However some applications are designed with workgroup computing in mind. Such applications can be set to mark alterations as 'revisions', highlighting any changes you make in a particular colour instead of updating the underlying document. At the end of the day such revisions can be accepted into the final document at its owner's discretion, or rejected. Alternatively, users may be able to add 'annotations' to the document containing pertinent comments.

Proper groupware can access the user's identity code, which they use when they first 'log-on' to the network, and use it as an electronic signature for their revisions and annotations. There are even project planning packages and personal information managers that can automatically schedule events by checking each participant's digital diary and booking the next time-slot when everyone will be available.

Conferencing

While e-mail is concerned with private messages, conferencing allows users to post messages to public storage areas for all to see. Conferencing systems are sometimes called bulletin board systems (BBS for short) because they are analogous to conventional bulletin boards, providing an area for public announcements and other shared messages.

Conferencing systems offer more than their conventional counterparts because they allow users to partake in conversations or 'threads', and can maintain many threads at the same time. Users can either comment on existing messages, or start new threads of their own. Conferencing systems can also divide the bulletin board into different areas or conferences, each concerned with a particular subject. Such conferences can be 'closed', in which case they are only available to select users, or 'open' so that anyone can join in.

Such a system can be extremely powerful. Conferences can be set up for every major project in the company, allowing the members of each team to keep up to date with the latest developments, without having to attend endless meetings. Furthermore, if the conference is open, the team can draw on the expertise of the whole company in a way that would never otherwise be feasible.

Conferencing can also be dangerous, particularly for those trying to protect a traditional management hierarchy. People tend to lose their inhibitions without face-to-face or voice contact, and conferences can easily become clogged with irrelevant nonsense. Such problems can be obviated by nominating a 'moderator' to take responsibility for each conference.

Electronic form management

As well as simple messages, a network makes a good vehicle for the forms that a business uses to manage its internal affairs. Electronic form management works in much the same way as conventional e-mail, but replaces the plain textual message with a more structured message that emulates the fields of the original form.

Dedicated software can then check that the required fields have been filled out by each user and route the form to its next port of call automatically. Many common business procedures, such as enquiry logging, stock management and so forth, can be automated using such a system.

Communications

So far we have looked at how a computer network can link computers within a company; however, that's only half the story. With suitable equipment you can put your computer in touch with the rest of the world bringing the benefits of:

- The global network
- On-line databases
- Electronic trading
- Teleworking
- Computer-telephone integration

This can be achieved either through the conventional telephone network or through special high-speed digital networks made available by telephone companies. The physical link to the external network is made through a piece of equipment called a 'modem' and is controlled by special communications software.

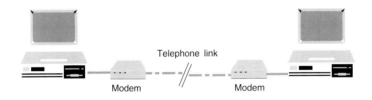

Telephone link

Modem   Modem

A modem can be connected to a local area network, giving all users on the network access to the outside world, or alternatively giving external users access to resources on the network. For such a system to work, the modem's machine needs to be running the appropriate communications server software, as discussed earlier.

An alternative to a simple modem is a fax/modem which can also receive fax messages, converting the fax data into bit-map images for your computer. Such an image can then be translated into text using OCR software.

The global network

There are thousands of computers throughout the world that can be accessed through a modem. Many provide services similar to those of a local area network, but on a global scale. Most ask for a membership fee, but once you are joined up you can take part in conferences and send e-mail to other members. Many also hold libraries of computer software that you can 'download' for use on your own system.

Over the years, many such computers have linked together to form a vast 'network of networks' known as the Internet. There are a wide variety of systems on the Internet, but most subscribe to a common e-mail addressing system and most carry Usenet. This is a vast conferencing system carrying discussions on almost every subject under the sun, both business and pleasure.

Originally the Internet was used almost exclusively by the academic community, but it is being used increasingly for business. The on-line community already numbers many millions of users, and is expanding all the time.

On-line databases

Another type of computer is the on-line database or 'information server'. These are large computer systems specifically set up to provide information to anyone who dials in with an appropriate password. Information on offer includes:

- Newspaper and magazine articles in abstract or full text form
- Library bibliographies that can be searched by title, subject, date, author or publication
- Up-to-the minute stock and share prices
- Company reports and data
- Scientific and medical papers
- Legal judgements

Most such databases charge membership fees based on the value of the data and the length of time you spend connected to the system. These charges may seem high but reflect the speed at which you can access data. If you know what you are doing then a couple of minutes on-line can be equivalent to many days trawling through a conventional library.

Electronic trading
Just as electronic form management can replace the paperwork that goes back and forth within a company, so Electronic Data Interchange, or EDI as it is called, can replace the flow of documents between companies. Instead of sending purchase orders, invoices statements and the like through the conventional post, EDI lets you send them as structured e-mail messages. No only does this cut down on the paperwork, it also means that your computer system can react automatically to the data in the message.

EDI requires considerable cooperation between participating companies, particularly as many of these documents represent legally binding transactions. Rather than set up the protocols themselves, most EDI users subscribe to one of the national EDI networks and let the network provider look after its own management.

Teleworking
Armed with a modem, suitable software and a decent telephone connection, anyone can 'dial in' to the network's communications server and log on just like any other user, even though they may be thousands of miles distant.

This has obvious benefits for company representatives whose jobs dictate that they spend most of their time out of the office. Using a portable computer and a modem, small enough to fit into a briefcase, they can log in from a hotel room, a client's office or even, with special equipment, through the cellular telephone network or by satellite link.

Many companies have also found it worthwhile to let employees work from home, should they wish, and even to provide them with the appropriate equipment.

Computer – telephone integration

Computer – telephone integration, or CTI, means connecting the computer network to the company's private telephone exchange so that phone calls can be controlled from the computer screen.

With the right equipment, phone messages can be stored on a special 'voice server'. When someone leaves a phone message the server sends an e-mail message to the appropriate user to tell them that a message is waiting. Users can then have the server play back their 'voice mail' through the internal phone system. Such a system can also provide Interactive Voice Response or Audiotex services, allowing callers to control the system using their telephone keypads.

Summary

Today we have looked at the various ways that computers can be connected together and at how networks can improve communication throughout your organisation. In particular, we have looked at:

- Electronic mail
- Document sharing
- Electronic conferencing
- Electronic form management
- Accessing global networks
- Using on-line databases
- Electronic trading
- Teleworking
- Integrating the telephone

Buying a system

Buying and installing a computer system has got to be one of the most traumatic activities known to man. As we saw in our introduction, information is the most valuable asset that a company has, which means that computerisation can either make or break a company. Fortunately, there are steps that you can take to reduce the likelihood of disaster:

Seven steps to painless installation

- Preparation
- Appoint a project manager
- Analyse your current procedures
- Specify your system needs
- Draw up a contract
- Appoint a supplier
- Test the system thoroughly

Preparation

Installing a new computer system is as much a human problem as a technical problem. What you are doing is replacing a collection of manual procedures, probably built up in a relatively haphazard fashion over many years, with what you hope are more efficient procedures centred around a carefully designed computer system. As far as your staff are concerned, you are redesigning their jobs.

However you approach it, the changeover is bound to cause disruption and insecurity. The effect can be minimised by ensuring that everyone concerned – not only staff but customers and suppliers as well – feel that the disruption will be worth while. For the staff in particular, this means involving them in the design process wherever possible.

The staff's major fear will be of redundancy, a fear which could well be borne out. Computers can indeed render jobs redundant, but in doing so, they could free someone to take up a more challenging post elsewhere within the company. Make sure this is a real possibility, rather than an empty promise.

Appoint a project manager

The first step is to appoint someone with sole responsibility for the system's purchase, installation and maintenance. It should ideally be someone already well known and respected within the organisation; someone sympathetic to the needs of the employees while remaining a firm believer in the benefits of the new system.

A large part of the project manager's job will concern the human side of the system, ensuring that the staff understand what is happening and appreciate the benefits that computers could bring. Having only one person in your company authorised to make decisions about the installation also makes life much easier for the system's supplier.

Analyse your current procedures

It may sound obvious, but before you can introduce a new computer system you need a clear understanding of how your current systems work.

The best way of gaining such an understanding is to ask your staff to tell you what they actually do, and show you the various forms and documents they use to carry out their tasks. This is where a systems analyst comes in handy, trained in the use of various techniques for analysing business systems.

Any business is a web of interacting processes, the output of one forming the input to another as information flows from employee to employee and department to department. Not all these process need to be transferred to computer, and indeed, careful system design can throw up more efficient manual solutions. It can be alarming to discover just how bureaucratic some of your existing practices have become.

An important part of the system designer's job is to define the 'boundary' of the proposed system, deciding which processes are to be computerised and what is to form the system's input and output. Only then can you draw up a meaningful specification.

Specify your system needs

If you are computerising your business from scratch then you would be well advised to employ an independent consultant to create a functional specification for the new system, and to interact with the actual suppliers on your behalf.

As its name suggests, a functional specification specifies what the system should be able to do, rather than detailing its actual components.

You may be fairly certain, for example, that a 120Mb hard disk is quite sufficient for your needs. If you actually specify a 120Mb hard disk and it proves woefully inadequate then you've only got yourself to blame. If, on the other hand, it was the supplier who suggested the 120Mb hard disk, then you've got a good case for an upgrade to something more suitable, free of charge.

In particular, a functional specification should make clear how fast the system must operate, and what volume of data it needs to handle – both now and in the future. If upgrading, make it clear that any new hardware or software needs to work with your existing system.

Draw up a contract

When you buy anything you enter into a contract with the supplier. In this country, the basis of the contract is the Sale of Goods Act which essentially states that goods should:

- Work
- Do what they are contracted to do
- Conform to their description

In addition to these implicit clauses, the contract can contain additional clauses that extend the rights or limit the liabilities of either party. These can be expressed verbally; however, it makes sense to put them in writing at the earliest opportunity.

The first two points in the Sale of Goods Act can be negated through exclusion clauses. However such clauses cannot exclude the supplier's obligation to describe the goods accurately, or the supplier's liability should the goods cause death or injury. Furthermore, it is usually up to the supplier to show that any exclusion clauses are 'reasonable'.

Most suppliers outline such clauses in their standard 'terms and conditions', which you should request at an early stage. Despite appearances, these are not carved in stone but should be treated as the starting point for your final contract. Read them carefully, and send them back with a covering letter explaining any changes you feel are necessary.

Your final contract may extend over several letters and documents sent back and forth. However, in its entirety it should cover the following points:

- What the system should do
- How long installation should take
- How much it will cost
- Compliance with EU directives
- Software licensing requirements
- Training and documentation
- Prototyping, user trials and alterations
- Future maintenance and updates

Obviously such an extensive contract is only necessary for the installation of a complete system, and even then your relationship with your supplier has to be based on trust, not contractual fine print. Nevertheless, elements of it are useful even if you are buying just a single PC or software package.

Compliance with EU directives

Members of the European Union are bound to implement the EU Directive concerning computer use in the office, which in the UK is embodied in the Health and Safety (Display Screen Equipment) Regulations 1992.

This lays down various requirements for the whole of an employee's environment, including not just the computer but the furniture, lighting and noise levels. It also specifies that software must be suitable for the task and easy to use. It is important that your new system conforms with these regulations.

Software licensing requirements

It is normal to purchase a licence to use computer software, rather than the software itself. This usually restricts the number of people who may use the software at any one time and on how many machines it may be installed, although it may be possible to buy a 'site licence' allowing unlimited use within the company. Make sure you have the right to assign your licence to a third party, perhaps in the event of a merger.

If the software has been written specifically for your business then you may wish the licence to be exclusive to yourselves, preventing the author from selling further copies to your competitors. You may also need some sort of protection against the author going into liquidation. One possibility is for the author to deposit the 'source code' (effectively the program's blueprint) with a third party.

Training and documentation
Training is an on-going part of system management which
we will cover tomorrow. Suffice it to say here that your
contract with the supplier should include provision for
adequate documentation and training.

Prototyping, user trials and alterations
It makes sense to build in regular progress meetings and
stages at which the system can be tested while under
development. If the installation involves purpose-built
software then its developer should be able to show you a
'prototype' system with just the user interface working. This
can be tested by the people who will actually be using it,
and modifications made at an early stage.

Once the system is finished there should be an 'acceptance
testing' period before it is deemed to be satisfactory and the
full sum paid over. Use this period to really test the system,
and in particular, its ability to handle large volumes of data
and large numbers of users without becoming unacceptably
slow.

Even after this acceptance period is up, you should
negotiate a further period during which any bugs that might
appear will be rectified free of charge.

Appoint a supplier

Where possible, buy your whole system from a single
supplier. Computer products are notoriously incompatible,
making it all too easy for the author of an application to
blame the operating system for any problems, and vice
versa. Buy both from the same source and the onus is on the
supplier to sort out such problems.

Mail order

If you know exactly what hardware or software you want, then you may well get the best price by buying through a catalogue or a magazine advertisement. If you do go this route, always check whether the goods are in stock and if not, agree a date by which they should be delivered.

Some magazines support a mail order protection scheme which will reimburse readers buying from an advertiser that goes into liquidation or becomes bankrupt before they have supplied you with the goods. Readers may need to register their purchase with the magazine first, and most magazines limit their overall liability to a stated value which means that readers will be reimbursed on a first-come-first-served basis.

Shops and superstores

If you prefer to check out the goods and the supplier first then a high-street shop or a superstore may be more suitable. Bear in mind that, despite appearances to the contrary, few such shops can offer in-depth advice.

VARs and consultancies

If you do need professional advice then go to either a value-added retailer (VAR) or a consultant. Value-added retailers add value to the goods that they sell by bundling them into complete systems, tailored to your business needs.

Most VARs specialise in a particular type of business and sell systems based around custom software that they have developed specifically for that market. Such software is called 'vertical market' software, and can often be adapted to your particular needs. This should be considerably cheaper than having a new system written from scratch.

A consultant will become as important to your business as your accountant or lawyer, and should ideally be independent of any particular manufacturer. As such they should act solely on your behalf, impartially choosing the equipment and services that best suit your needs. Unfortunately many have vested interests.

The best way to find a consultant is through personal recommendation. Alternatively, look for someone who asks questions about your business, and responds to your questions in a language that you understand.

After-sales support

Once your system is installed and working you need to be confident that any problems it might develop are fixed quickly and properly. A large system may merit a support team on the premises, which we will look at tomorrow. However, even they will need help from the manufacturers on occasion, and this is best established at the time of purchase.

Most software publishers provide telephone support and some offer a whole range of support services, including on-line conferences and regular newsletters. In a similar vein, most hardware manufacturers offer maintenance contracts after the initial warranty period is over.

Dealing with problems

Most problems arise because of a misunderstanding and can be cleared up relatively amicably. Occasionally, however, you may need to resort to the law.

Consumer legislation varies from country to country, but in the UK it hinges on the contract that exists between the customer and the supplier. Note that the supplier is the company that actually sells you the goods, and not the manufacturer, unless you buy direct. Indeed if you enter into a hire-purchase agreement then, as far as the law is concerned, the finance company becomes the supplier.

In the event that either side fails to fulfil its obligations, the contract can either be rescinded or terminated, and the innocent party becomes entitled to compensation. If the contract is rescinded, you will be able to recover all money paid to the supplier to date. If, on the other hand, you can show that the supplier is guilty of misrepresentation or negligence, you may be entitled to substantial damages as well. In either case you should seek the advice of an expert.

If you do need to take legal advice, choose a solicitor that has a computer law group. Alternatively, look for a consultancy that specialises in computer litigation and loss assessment.

Provided your company is not incorporated, you can gain further protection under the Consumer Credit Act by purchasing with a credit card or through a credit agreement. If certain conditions are met, the credit company then becomes equally liable with the supplier in the event of a problem:

Conditions
- The cost of the goods is over £100 and not more than £30 000 including VAT
- Not more than £15 000 credit has been advanced
- The credit has been advanced through an existing arrangement between the supplier and the credit company

Incorporated companies do not have the same protection, and indeed the legal situation becomes rather more complicated if a finance company is involved.

How to handle a problem

- Stop using the goods and phone the supplier at once. Take a note of the person's name, what they say, and the time and date
- If you don't get immediate satisfaction, write to the supplier describing the problem in full. Attach photocopies of any relevant documents and receipts
- If your problem concerns a misleading trade description or goods that have proved unsafe, contact your local Trading Standards or Consumer Protection Department
- If your company is not incorporated and the goods were purchased on credit, write to the credit company telling them of your problem and that you intend to stop payments until it is sorted out
- If you feel that you have lost substantial business as a result of the problem, talk to a specialist in computer litigation before proceeding further

Summary

By now you should be armed against some of the pitfalls of computer installation, thanks to the 'Seven Steps to Painless Installation' that we introduced this morning.

In particular, you should be ready to analyse how your organisation currently operates, and to involve your staff in the design of the planned installation. You should also be on the way to drafting a contract with your supplier that will ensure a trouble-free relationship.

Managing a system

As we saw yesterday, installing a new computer system is as much about designing jobs as it is about hardware and software. Groupware, and in particular electronic form management, can turn your existing procedures upside down. It is obviously vital that your staff understand right from the start exactly what the new procedures are, and how the system works. If they don't, a minor hiccup could develop into a full-blown disaster as panic takes hold. For these reasons, it is best to set up a support team.

Support team

The project manager, whom we appointed yesterday, is the natural person to take responsibility for the system once it is installed. It is important that this be made official, and that he or she be allowed to recruit a team of suitable size. Every company should have at least one person with specific responsibility for system support, while larger organisations will need a separate IT department. This support team has a number of responsibilities:

- Hardware and software maintenance
- Documenting procedures
- Training the staff in system use
- Maintaining data security
- Ensuring software licences are not breached
- Keeping abreast of technological developments

Documenting procedures

The first step towards establishing a new set of procedures is proper documentation. By rights, this should be generated hand in hand with the system itself. All too often it is left to the programmers who wait until the system is finished, by which time they are far too closely involved to describe it in terms that your staff can understand.

Documentation should be written specifically for the people who will be using the system. Where you have used off-the-shelf rather than purpose-built software, it is all too easy to rely on the various manuals provided by the manufacturers. These may well be produced to a high standard, but nevertheless they should only ever supplement documentation written specifically to the needs of your company.

Ideally, each person likely to use the system should be given documents covering the following points, many of which we will be looking at more closely later today:

- Day-to-day operation of the system
- Data backup procedures
- Preventing virus infection
- Staying within the Data Protection Act
- Preventing a breach of software licence
- What to do if the system misbehaves
- How to get hold of system managers

In addition, it is important that each manager should be aware of their staff's training requirements and their rights under EU Directives. In particular, all staff are entitled to regular eye tests at their employer's expense, and to a free pair of spectacles or contact lenses should they prove necessary as a result of working with computer equipment.

Training

Your staff will generally need training in three specific areas:

- General use of the computer
- Using specific applications
- New office procedures

and there are three main methods of training delivery:

- In-house
- Computer based
- Outside courses

It is absolutely essential that you make provision for proper training within the office schedule. Without it, your staff may muddle through, giving up their own free time to study the manuals and work out how it all works, but the result is bound to be less efficient and could easily end up in disaster. Proper training is almost always cost effective.

In-house training
Of course, many will already be familiar with general computer use, either from earlier work experience or because they have a computer at home. Conversely, there may be some people who do not feel at all comfortable in front of a keyboard and screen. It is important that such people be allowed time to simply play with the system, without pressure to produce useful work.

HELLO? HELLO?

It is for this reason that some operating systems come with a few simple games, allowing users to get familiar with the mouse and the various elements of the user interface in a relaxed manner.

If you are lucky, some of the more experienced staff members may naturally fall into the role of informal teachers. Such people can be identified by the cries of, 'Hey Sam, how do I get the computer to do this...?' that go up whenever they appear in the office.

It is worth cultivating such people by making the role official and adjusting their work load so that they can fulfil it properly. Make sure that they are conversant with the correct procedures, and are known to the support team.

Computer-based training

Computer-based training has become increasingly viable with most major software packages providing an on-screen tutorial that uses the software itself to show new users how to carry out various operations. There are also special training packages available, designed specifically to train users at various levels of experience.

Such software can be highly effective, particularly as it lets users train at their own speed and set their own schedule. That said, it is still important to set aside specific periods for training, and to make sure these periods are free from interruptions. There is nothing like a constantly ringing phone to detract from the benefits that such sessions can bring.

Outside courses

There are plenty of training companies that specialise in computers and computer software. Many offer the option of courses either on their premises or on-site, whichever suits you best. They may even be able to tailor the course towards the documents and procedures used by your organisation, particularly if you are going to use them on a regular basis.

In general, a good course should offer the following:

- A tutor who is interesting and well-versed in the subject being taught
- One computer per user, and a spare should anything go wrong
- Purpose-written notes that can be taken away when the course is finished for reference in the office
- More hands-on experience than passive listening
- Time set aside at the end of the session for answering questions
- A quiet and comfortable environment

Your support team will have different training requirements to the rest of your staff, and will probably require more frequent training. Make sure that any training is relevant to the task in hand, and that staff are able to practise what they have learnt as soon as they finish the course, otherwise their training will be wasted.

Maintaining data security

The longer a computer system is in use, the more valuable
your data becomes. No computer system is infallible,
although hopefully any major bugs will become apparent
early on and will be covered by your contract with the
supplier. However it makes sense to keep both your old
manual procedures and the new system going in parallel for
a period, just in case.

Computer systems are vulnerable to traditional disasters,
such as fire or vandalism, as well as more hi-tech problems
such as virus infection. Procedures need to be in place to
both prevent and to cope with such possibilities.

Data backup
One obvious security measure is not to keep all your data in
one place but to make regular copies which are stored
elsewhere. This is called 'backing up' your data. It is
absolutely vital that you instigate proper backup
procedures, and that your staff are aware of their
importance.

Most operating systems include backup utilities, and there
are numerous independent products available as well. Most
will allow you to either take a full backup, copying
everything on to the hard disk, or an incremental backup
that copies just those files that have changed since the last
full backup.

There are various backup regimes that you can use,
depending on the importance of the data. Most
organisations are going to have their most important data
on the file server, so it is here that the most strict regime

should be adopted. It also makes sense to use a tape backup system for the file server, rather than floppy disk. A suitable regime involving a number of tapes might be:

- Full backup every week on to each tape in rotation
- Incremental backup taken each day
- Backup tapes stores in fire-proof safe
- Backup for the previous week stored off-site
- Oldest tapes replaced each month and archived

Make sure that everyone knows at what time the backups take place, and logs off the network while it is conducted. Alternatively, many backup utilities allow you to schedule backups for quiet periods, such as the early hours of the morning.

It may also be worth encouraging users to take responsibility for their own data, if only to the extent of copying their current documents onto a floppy disk. This does incur a security risk, but it might save a lot of anguish if the system does go wrong.

Viruses and hackers

If you are to believe the more sensationalist organs of the media, computer systems stand besieged by evil hackers armed to the teeth with lethal computer viruses. Needless to say, this is a distorted view of the true situation.

Technically, a computer virus is simply a program designed to copy itself on to as many systems as possible. Most also deliver some sort of 'payload' which can range from a simple 'look how clever I am' message to rendering your hard disk completely useless. The important point is that the payload is usually delivered after the virus has had plenty of time to spread, so it is unlikely to make its presence felt until your system has been infected for some time.

Many viruses are little more than harmless pranks, however some can be deadly. The most dangerous take time to make small changes to your data, sometimes over several months, before making themselves known.

Although viruses are very rare, it is worth taking basic precautions. In particular, there are antivirus utilities that you can use to check every disk and file that is put into the system, and provide tools for dealing with an infection should it occur.

Many viruses make changes to the operating system itself, usually to prevent themselves being discovered. For this reason it is worth keeping a 'clean' copy on a separate floppy disk that has its 'write protect' tab set so that its contents can't be changed. That way you can always establish a clean environment from which to deal with the infection.

Your system can only be attacked if the virus or the hacker can gain access, either directly through a machine on the network or through a modem link. Direct access is usually restricted by not letting anyone on the system unless a correct password is entered against a user's name. However, this only works if the passwords themselves are secure. It is this name/password combination that identifies users to the system, so your staff need to be aware of its importance and of the need to keep their password secure.

Viruses can only get into a system if someone puts them there, usually by inserting an infected floppy disk. One solution is to use workstations that don't have floppy disk drives at all, so that all software has to be loaded from the file server. Otherwise, make sure that users are aware that they should not use any foreign floppy disks without express permission from the system manager.

If you do connect to the telephone system, think very carefully about who might gain access. Some communications software supports a technique called 'call-back'. This stores a list of authorised users on the dial-in machine, together with the telephone numbers of their modems. As soon as a remote user calls in and issues the correct password, the system disconnects and then dials the user back on the listed number. Although not infallible, call-back does add an extra level of security.

Another solution is to provide a separate dial-up system altogether, disconnected from the main network. A more sophisticated approach is to set up a 'fire wall' that filters the flow of data between the dial-up system and the organisation's internal network.

If you do suffer a major attack or infection you would do better to call in an expert than try and tackle it internally. Meanwhile, it is worth taking basic precautions:

Basic security measures
- Install a virus scanner on every computer
- Keep a 'clean' copy of the operating system
- Scan all disks coming into the organisation for viruses
- Make sure passwords are difficult to guess
- Get users to change their passwords regularly
- Restrict physical access to the file server itself
- Restrict user access to necessary directories
- Establish a regime of regular backups
- Keep backups locked up – they contain valuable data

In practice, you are more likely to suffer an attack from a disgruntled employee than from a teenage hacker. Make sure that the system is physically secure, and in particular that the file server itself is in a locked room. Most network operating systems allow you to restrict user access to particular files or directories. Granting access to a directory on the file server is equivalent to giving someone a key to a locked room, so treat it with the same caution.

Software auditing

It makes sense to periodically catalogue all the software on your system, both to ensure compliance with your software licences and to identify unauthorised programs. Carrying out a software audit is an arduous task, but there are utilities specifically designed for the purpose. Furthermore, if your staff know that such audits take place they may think twice before installing their own potentially virus-infected software.

Insurance

Most insurance companies will insure computer equipment against the usual hazards of fire, accident and theft, and some also offer policies to cover you against data loss. Such policies may cover you for both the cost of recovering the data and the income lost as a result. If such policies seem expensive, remember that your data is probably many times more valuable than the equipment itself.

Data Protection Act

If you use your computer system to store details about people then you may well have to register its use with the Data Protection Registrar. Under the Data Protection Act you are obliged to keep such data secure, and to provide access to those whose details you store.

The Act states that you do not have to register data relating solely to payroll, pension or accounting, or simple name and address files unless inclusion implies additional information. A 'bad debtor' list would need to be registered, for example, even if it only contains names and addresses.

Summary

Keeping a system up and running is vital to the operation of your organisation. As we have seen today, the keys to managing a computer system are:

- Appoint a permanent support team
- Document all procedures
- Ensure adequate training
- Establish a regime for regular data back-up
- Take measures to maintain security
- Take out adequate insurance
- Register your data if appropriate

Preparing for the future

The chances are that your computer system will be out of date almost as soon as it is installed, but you may at least be able to avoid the most obvious blind alleys by keeping an eye on the future. Today, we are going to look at a few of the changes and technologies that are likely to become commonplace over the next few years, and their implications.

- Multimedia
- The information highway
- Teleworking
- The user interface
- Pocket communicators
- A sea of objects

Multimedia

At the time of writing, most personal computers have limited capabilities when it comes to sight and sound, although they can usually be upgraded to the point where they can reproduce photographic quality images and hi-fi quality audio without too great an expense. Full-motion video of any quality still requires specialised equipment, making it practical only for those directly involved in the media.

At present, standard desktop computers simply aren't powerful enough to cope with the amount of data required to refresh a high-definition display 25 or 30 times a second. However, this will change, and in a few years' time every desktop computer will be capable of manipulating and displaying full-screen video of at least TV quality, in much the same way as it can handle still images and sound today.

Of course this doesn't mean that we will all have to become film directors. What it will mean is a blurring of the distinction between the world of computers and the world of video. Video recorders will play CDs rather than tapes, and those CDs will be compatible with your computer's CD-ROM drive. CD-ROM could well become the standard medium for all video, whether feature film, training programme, business presentation or home movie.

It will also mean that video messaging becomes as commonplace as voice messaging is at the moment. Every computer on a network could easily be equipped with a miniature video camera that allows users to record and mail video messages to each other. This may sound frivolous, however research has shown that such 'video conferencing' facilities can enhance the effectiveness of a team.

The information highway

The last few years have seen a considerable increase in the use of wide-area computer networks, particularly the Internet.

Furthermore, most of the major communications companies are jostling to establish high-speed data networks capable of handling even the volumes of data required for full-motion video. There is much talk, even at government level, about 'information highways', or communications networks that could revolutionise our society in much the same way as the roads did at the beginning of this century.

Such networks would mean that any computer in the world would be as easy to access as your local file server. In the long run this could well blur the distinction between one machine and another.

The problems that need to be overcome before this becomes reality are as much commercial and political as technical. Protocols have to be agreed for ensuring the smooth transfer of information between disparate systems, and for maintaining security. Such a free flow of information also has implications as far as copyright and ownership of data are concerned.

Teleworking

Perhaps the biggest impact that such an information highway will have will be on our perception of employment. There has already been a shift away from employees who work for a particular company for most of their lives and expect the company to make some provision for their old age. Instead, managers are increasingly offering temporary contracts to people with the skills to carry out a particular job, a process known as 'outsourcing'.

The increased power of personal computers and the rise of information highways can only encourage such trends. Already we are seeing 'virtual offices' and 'virtual companies' created solely for a specific project, and dissolved when the work is done. Such offices may span continents, identified only by an e-mail address and a common purpose.

These trends have a number of implications. For the manager, it brings added flexibility and lessens their responsibility for the long-term welfare of the staff. However, managers cannot expect the same degree of loyalty from people who might be working for a competitor once their contract is finished. Such considerations also reduce the incentive to provide training.

For the 'teleworker' there is also added flexibility and freedom, but teleworkers have to provide for their own insurance and pension needs, and sometimes supply their own tools of the trade. Furthermore, international data highways mean that they may find themselves competing for work on the world market, against people operating from very different cost bases. Indeed such technologies have profound implications for our society as a whole.

The user interface

The way that we use our computers is also likely to change. At the moment, most people still use a 'qwerty' keyboard, a device designed over a century ago in order to slow down typists who were typing too fast for their mechanical typewriters. While the keyboard is likely to stick around for some time yet, it won't be long before voice becomes the most common way of controlling your computer.

The mouse is also likely to be replaced by a more direct form of touch, either through the finger or, where more precision is required, using a pen or pencil. The end result is a machine that we communicate with in much the same way as we would another human being, and indeed such a computer may well display a human face as a focal point.

Voice recognition is feasible even now, although it is expensive. What is more difficult is natural language processing, or the ability to turn vague instructions into precise commands that the computer can act upon. Eventually our computers will be able to adopt distinct personalities, and even a modicum of 'common sense'.

We will certainly need their assistance if we are to navigate the vast seas of information that the data highways will open up for us. This is where the idea of a 'software agent' comes in, roving the world's networks for information relevant to our affairs, and reporting back whenever they dig up something interesting.

Pocket communicators
Increased access to global networks, coupled with intelligent user interfaces able to cope with voice and touch, will make pocket-sized computers far more practical. Such a 'pocket communicator' or 'personal digital assistant' (PDA for short) may not carry a great deal of data itself, but will instead provide a portable interface to the network through telephone, radio or even satellite link from anywhere in the world. They could well replace the notebook computers that we use today.

A sea of objects
Going behind the user interface, the whole relationship between applications and data is also undergoing a change. Instead of mammoth slabs of software, packing all the features you could possibly need into one monolithic package, applications are likely to become bundles of loosely connected tools that can be used in different combinations, and even with tools from other manufacturers.

Each tool will cater for a particular need, so there may be one tool for editing text, another for checking spelling, and yet another for handling tabular data. At the moment, many applications provide a 'macro' language that allows you to alter the way they work, customising them to suit the task at hand. Already we are seeing the development of common macro languages, understood by all applications, which will enable you to group software tools into new combinations tailored specifically to the needs of your company.

Such tools are often referred to as 'objects', because they have specific properties and can be manipulated in well-defined ways. A drawing tool might have a 'shape' property, for example that can be set to 'square' or 'circle'.

In a world of high-speed networks, such tools need not live on the same machine (which is why some people have started to talk about a 'sea of objects') available to anyone in any combination that they find useful. Eventually the distinction between applications and data will disappear altogether, and you will be able to work directly on a document. You will no longer need to consider the software that you happen to be using, leaving the computer to make sure that you have the appropriate tool for the job.